SPOTLIGHT ON SOCCER

THE BUSINESS OF SOCCER

Clive Gifford

PowerKiDS press
New York

Published in 2011 by The Rosen Publishing Group Inc.
29 East 21st Street, New York, NY 10010

First Edition

Editor: Julia Adams
Produced by: Tall Tree Ltd.
Editor, Tall Tree: Jon Richards
Designer: Ben Ruocco

Library of Congress Cataloging-in-Publication Data

Gifford, Clive.
The business of soccer / Clive Gifford. -- 1st ed.
p. cm. -- (Spotlight on soccer)
Includes index.
ISBN 978-1-61532-610-5 (library binding)
ISBN 978-1-61532-615-0 (paperback)
ISBN 978-1-61532-619-8 (6-pack)
1. Soccer--Social aspects--Juvenile literature.
2. Soccer--Management--Juvenile literature. I. Title.
GV943.25.G538 2011
796.334--dc22

2009045778

Photographs
t—top, l—left, r—right, b—bottom, c—center
cover t—Dreamstime.com/Berlinfoto, tr—Dreamstime.com/Photoplanet, br—Dreamstime.com/Benjamincoppens, bl—Dreamstime.com/Chunni4691, tl—Dreamstime.com/Diademimages, c—Dreamstime.com/Josefbosak, 1 Dreamstime.com/Albo, 2 Dreamstime.com/Diademimages, 4 Dreamstime.com/Matt Trommer, 5 Dreamstime.com/Camhi Franck, 6 Dreamstime.com/Andrea Presazzi, 7 Dreamstime.com/Diademimages, 8 Dreamstime.com/Diademimages, 9 Dreamstime.com/Robert Howarth, 10 Eddie Keogh/Reuters/Corbis, 11 Matthew Ashton/AMA/Corbis, 12 Dreamstime.com/Kojoku, 13 Dreamstime.com/Mitchell Gunn, 14 Dreamstime.com/Albo, 15 Ben Radford/Corbis, 16 Dreamstime.com/Diademimages, 17 Ben Radford/Corbis, 18 Dreamstime.com/Mitchell Gunn, 19 istockphoto.com/Dan Barnes, 20 Matthias Schrader/epa/Corbis, 21 Catherine Ivill/AMA/Corbis, 22 Stephane Reix/For Picture/Corbis, 23 Stephane Reix/TempSport/Corbis, 24 Matthew Ashton/AMA/Corbis, 25 Peter Morgan/Reuters/Corbis, 26 Ahmad Yusni/epa/Corbis, 27 Dreamstime.com/Ken Durden, 28 Ciro Fusco/epa/Corbis, 29 Dreamstime.com/Melissad10, 30 Matt Brown/isiphotos.com/Corbis, 32 Dreamstime.com/Diademimages

Acknowledgements
The author and publisher would like to thank the following people for their help and participation in this book: Whiteknights FC, Eric Burrow, Steve Rendell, and Paul Scholey.

Manufactured in China.
CPSIA Compliance Information: Batch #WAS0102PK: For Further Information contact Rosen Publishing, New York, New York at 1-800-237-9932

CONTENTS

The World's Game

Soccer is the world's most popular team sport. It is played and watched by hundreds of millions of people who are attracted to its constant action, moments of drama, and the skills of its players.

Business Beginnings

When soccer developed in Britain in the mid-1800s, it was an amateur sport played mainly for fun. As the game increased in popularity, players were initially paid expenses for travel and then for time away from work. Gradually, soccer players became professional, paid to play the sport full-time. At first, their salaries were funded by fans paying to watch their heroes play. As soccer has boomed, millions of fans are drawn to watch matches live at soccer grounds or on television, and this generates large sums of money. This money has seen certain clubs grow into giants, and top players have become global stars and multimillionaires.

ON THE BALL

In 1871, teams paid £1 ($127 today) to play in the first major cup competition, the English FA Cup. In the 2008-09 season, winners received £2 million ($3.6 million).

Players from Real Madrid celebrate winning the 2007–08 Spanish league title. Winning league and cup competitions provides clubs with large sums of money.

Brazilian soccer fans watch a game between Botafogo and Flamengo at the Maracanã stadium in Rio de Janeiro, Brazil, in 2008. Soccer in South America is controlled by the *Confederación Sudamericana de Fútbol* (South American Football Confederation), or CONMEBOL.

Organizing Soccer

In 1904, the *Fédération International de Football Association* (FIFA) was formed with just seven member countries (France, Belgium, Denmark, the Netherlands, Spain, Sweden, and Switzerland). Today, FIFA has more than 200 member countries and runs soccer around the world. This includes the planet's biggest tournament, the World Cup. Each continent also has its own organization that runs competitions. In Europe, the Union of European Football Associations (UEFA) runs competitions such as the European Championships and the Champions League. In Asia, the Asian Football Confederation (AFC) runs the Asian Champions League. Africa's organizing body is the Confederation of African Football (CAF), and it runs the African Champions League for clubs and the African Cup of Nations for national teams.

> ***"I take pride in the fact that people go home having felt that for 90 minutes today, life is beautiful and that's it, basically. That's why professional football [soccer] exists."***
>
> Manager of Arsenal, **Arsene Wenger**

The Soccer Industry

Soccer today is a sport dominated by money. The biggest clubs need money to buy the best players so that they can become more successful. They raise money from fans and from commercial agreements.

The Big Leagues

All of the 20 richest clubs, except Fenerbahçe in Turkey, are found in the world's five biggest leagues. These are the German *Bundesliga*, the French *Le Championnat*, the English *Premier League*, *Serie A* in Italy, and *La Liga* in Spain. There is much less money in women's soccer, with most female players earning only part of their income from playing soccer. There are professional female leagues in Germany, Sweden, and from 2009, Women's Professional Soccer (WPS) in the United States.

ON THE BALL

In May 2008, the most valuable game in soccer saw Hull City beat Bristol City. Hull won promotion to the English Premier League and £60 million ($108 million) in payments.

Players of AC Milan (in red), one of the richest clubs in the world, take on Udinese in the Italian Serie A league in 2008.

The Rest of the World

Elsewhere, soccer leagues are booming in popularity, especially in the United States, China, Japan, and South Korea. African and South American leagues continue to produce top-class soccer players, but clubs struggle to keep hold of them. Many of the world's best players are not European, but come from South America, Asia, and Africa. These players are drawn to play for clubs in Europe, attracted by high salaries and the chance to play against other top players.

Money Box

Richest clubs by income, 2007–08

1. Real Madrid (Spain)	$521.3 million
2. Manchester Utd (England)	$480.8 million
3. Barcelona (Spain)	$440 million
4. Bayern Munich (Germany)	$420.8 million
5. Chelsea (England)	$383.2 million
6. Arsenal (England)	$376.7 million
7. Liverpool (England)	$300.6 million
8. AC Milan (Italy)	$298.4 million
9. AS Roma (Italy)	$250 million
10. Internazionale (Italy)	$246.4 million

Source: *Deloitte Football Money League*, 2009

Two players contest a ball during a 2008 Major League Soccer (MLS) match between D.C. United (in black) and Toronto FC. Since it started in 1996, MLS has spread its business base from ten teams in just one country to 15 teams in both the United States and Canada.

Soccer Fans

Soccer teams rely on fans to support them during matches and to raise money. Fans contribute to a club by paying for tickets to watch games and by buying club merchandise, such as replica shirts.

Club Soccer

During a season (all the games played in one year), fans will travel all over a country to follow their club in action away from their home stadium. Many fans will also buy a season ticket costing hundreds of dollars. This allows them to go to all the matches in their team's own stadium. These matches are known as home games. With match ticket prices costing up to $100, soccer clubs can raise a lot of money from selling tickets, especially if they can attract crowds of more than 50,000 fans to each game.

Italian fans celebrate winning a match during the Euro 2008 finals. The money raised from ticket and merchandise sales from international matches goes to international bodies, such as UEFA, and national organizations.

Supporters' Clubs

Most clubs have supporters' clubs that organize tickets and travel to games. Bayern Munich, for example, has more than 2,000 club branches with more than 132,000 paying members, making it the most organized supported club in Germany. All of the money raised from fans can make up a large part of a club's income. In the case of small clubs, money from fans may be the only source of income. Larger clubs are able to raise money from other sources, such as television and sponsorship.

For the 1998-99 season, Beryl Owen made the 435 mile (700 km) trip from her home to the St. James Park stadium, Newcastle, UK, for every match, even though she could not get a ticket.

An upset fan sits alone after his team has lost. Even if a team is performing poorly, fans will still pay a lot of money to support it. During the 2008–09 season, for example, the average cost of an English Premier League season ticket was $1,062.

Money Box

Top Major League Soccer (MLS) average attendance

CLUB	YEAR	FANS PER GAME
1 Seattle Sounders	2009	30,943
2 L.A. Galaxy	1996	28,916
3 L.A. Galaxy	2008	26,009
4 L.A. Galaxy	2007	24,252
5 L.A. Galaxy	2005	24,204
6 MetroStars	1996	23,898
7 L.A. Galaxy	2004	23,809
8 L.A. Galaxy	2003	21,983
9 L.A. Galaxy	1998	21,784
10 D.C. United	2001	21,518
11 NE Revolution	1997	21,423

Club Owners

Soccer club owners are responsible for the business side of a club. Their roles will vary from club to club, but they may be involved in negotiating contracts with sponsors or agreeing fees to buy players.

Forms of Ownership

Soccer clubs are owned in lots of ways. Some sell shares on stock exchanges and are owned by the shareholders who appoint a board to run the club. Others are owned by thousands of members. Clubs such as Barcelona and Real Madrid in Spain and Yokohama FC in Japan have elections every few years where their members vote on who should run the club. In Mexico, the media company Televisa owns not only the national stadium, the Azteca, but also three major soccer clubs: San Luis FC, Club América, and Club Necaxa. In 2008, an offer to buy Club Necaxa for around $23.4 million came from the Mexican state government of Aguascalientes.

Some clubs are owned by very wealthy individuals. The Russian oil tycoon, Roman Abramovich, bought the English Premier League club Chelsea in 2003 for $252 million and has spent more than $360 million on players.

ON THE BALL

Philip Anschutz of the United States owns stakes in three clubs: the L.A. Galaxy and Houston Dynamo in the MLS, as well as Hammarby in Sweden.

Taking Over a Club

Soccer clubs regularly change owners. In recent years, the English Premier League clubs Liverpool, Manchester United, and Aston Villa have all been taken over by U.S. businessmen. Manchester City was first bought by the former Prime Minister of Thailand, Thaksin Shinawatra, and then, in 2008, by the ruling family of Abu Dhabi. Clubs from lower leagues have also attracted new owners who are anxious to buy a team for a lot less money than a top-flight club. In 2007, the English Championship club, Queens Park Rangers (QPR), changed owners. It is now owned by Lakshmi Mittal, the fifth-richest man in the world, and Formula One bosses Bernie Ecclestone and Flavio Briatore.

> *"I see it as part of my role as chairman to make sure we have the maximum funds . . . to be as competitive as possible. It is my duty to be on the lookout for investors."*
>
> Chairperson of Tranmere Rovers, **Lorraine Rogers**

QPR owners Lakshmi Mittal (second from left) and Flavio Briatore (third from left) stand alongside former QPR players (from left to right) Gerry Francis, Les Ferdinand, and Paul Parker at a ceremony to unveil the club's new badge in 2008.

Managers and Coaches

The person in charge of a team is called a manager or coach. Both coaches and managers are involved in training players for matches. Managers, however, are also involved in some of the business aspects of a club, such as buying and selling players.

ON THE BALL

Christoph Daum, manager of the German team, Bayer Leverkusen, once asked his team to walk barefoot over broken glass as part of an exercise in positive thinking.

The Merry-go-round

Managers and coaches are vital to the success of a team. They decide who plays and what tactics to use. These are key to how successful a team will become—the more games a club wins, the more prize money it collects and the more fans come to see it play, earning the club even more money. The pressures to succeed at the biggest clubs are immense, and if a coach is unsuccessful, they may be dismissed by their club.

Since 1990, Real Madrid has had 13 different managers, including Gus Hiddink (left), who went on to manage Australia, South Korea, and Russia.

Head of a Team

A manager or coach will be the head of a large staff at a club. This staff will include skills and fitness coaches who train the squad as well as reserve and youth teams. Physical therapists treat injured players, and nutritionists look after players' diets. Some managers also employ other experts. Luiz Felipe Scolari, former manager of Brazil, Portugal, and the English club, Chelsea, has employed the same sports psychologist, Regina Brandao, for his teams for the past 12 years.

> ***"The most important person in any club is the manager. They make or break it. If they buy the wrong players, or get them playing the wrong way, they bankrupt you."***
>
> Managing Director of Birmingham City, **Karren Brady**

The coaching team of Manchester United during the 2008 Champions League final. For the 2008–09 season, manager Sir Alex Ferguson (third from right) led a team of 16 coaching staff, including goalkeeping coaches, scouts, and team doctors.

The Stadium and Staff

Owning a large soccer stadium means that a club can attract thousands of paying fans to watch matches. However, a stadium is expensive to build and maintain, and needs hundreds of workers to run it.

Moving Grounds

As soccer has boomed in popularity, many clubs move away from old stadiums to bigger, more modern grounds. The English Premier League team Arsenal moved a short distance in London from their 38,419-seat Highbury ground to the new 60,432-seat Emirates stadium. Other teams have moved farther afield in search of new fans—the English team Wimbledon, moved 68 miles (110 km) from London to Milton Keynes in 2003 to attract more fans to watch games.

ON THE BALL

The biggest-ever match crowd occurred during the 1950 World Cup when 199,850 people crammed into the Maracanã Stadium in Rio de Janeiro, Brazil.

Some teams share a large stadium in order to save on costs. The Italian Serie A clubs, AC Milan and Internazionale, share the 85,000-seater San Siro stadium.

> *The football [soccer] ground is my arena, my colosseum, and it doesn't matter if I am fighting lions or men, I feel like I am the gladiator.*
>
> Siena striker,
> **Massimo Maccarone**

Club Workers

A stadium needs many people to run it on match day, from stewards who deal with seating, to staff selling tickets at the box office. Away from the game, a club is a major business, employing people to market and promote the club, run its web site, handle its finances, and organize the sales of shirts and other souvenirs. Grounds keepers look after both the stadium's field and the fields at the training ground, and visitor tours of a club's stadium are often led by famous ex-players. Many clubs will also finance and run programs for young and disadvantaged people in their local communities.

A groundskeeper uses a blower to dry the markings on a pitch before a match at the Luzhniki Stadium in Moscow, Russia. Hundreds of people are employed to make sure that each game of soccer goes safely and efficiently.

Moneymakers

In 1999, Fiorentina offered fans cans containing air from its stadium. These were called "Essence of Victory," "Dressing Room Atmosphere," and "Air of the Terraces."

Top soccer clubs earn their money from three areas. These are selling the television rights to show matches, revenue from ticket sales, and income from commercial activities, such as merchandising and sponsorship.

Commercial Revenue

Commercial staff at a club work hard to maximize the club's income. A stadium may be used to hold rock concerts, and luxurious box seating is sold to companies who wish to entertain guests at a live match.

Soccer clubs also try to persuade companies to spend large sums of money buying blocks of seats at their grounds, and to advertise inside the stadiums and on the players' shirts.

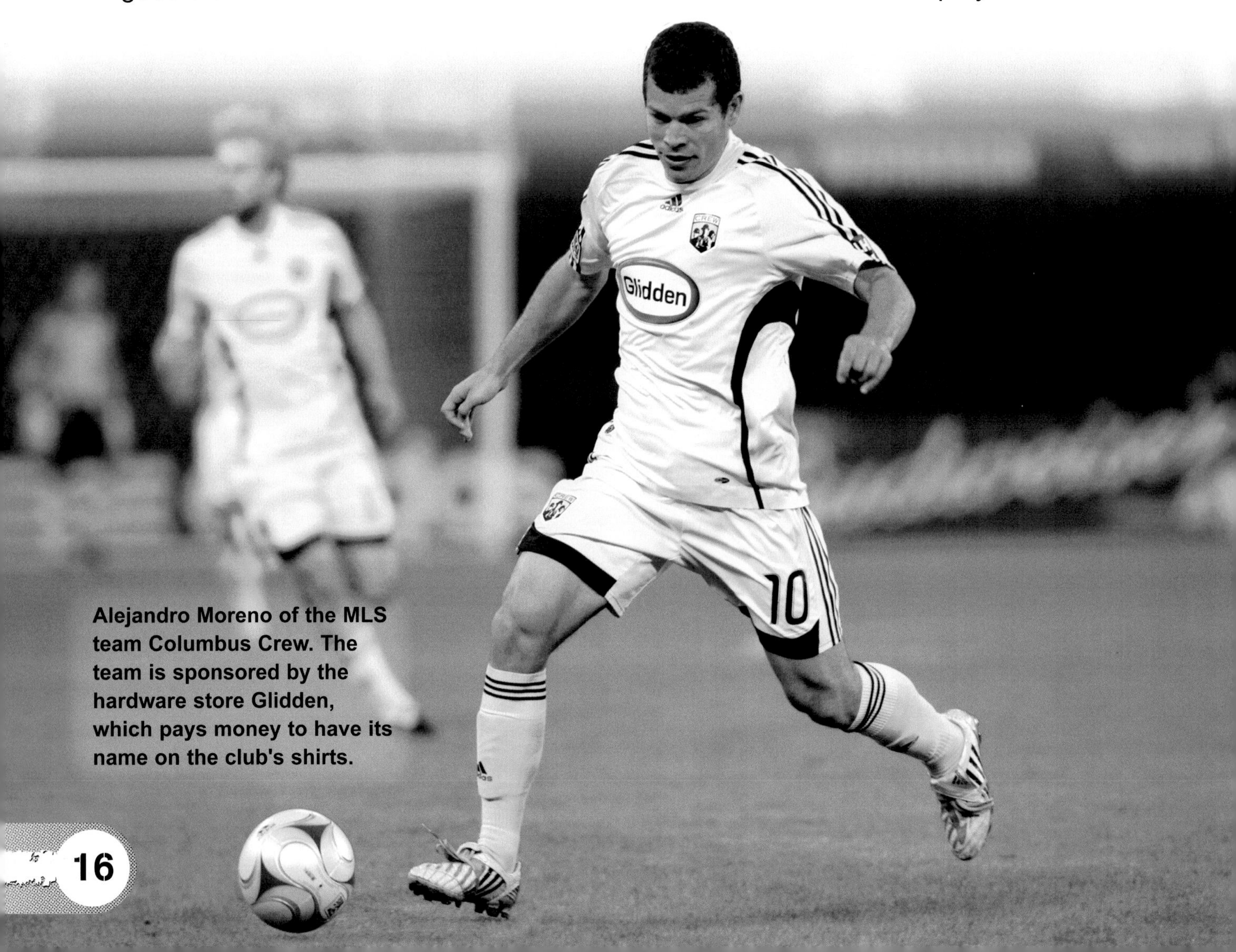

Alejandro Moreno of the MLS team Columbus Crew. The team is sponsored by the hardware store Glidden, which pays money to have its name on the club's shirts.

The French national soccer coach, Raymond Domenech, browses through Manchester United merchandise. Clubs will put their names, colors, and logos on a wide range of merchandise, including replica shirts and baby clothes.

Matchday and Merchandise

The money that fans pay to enter the stadium and watch the game can be a major part of the income a soccer club receives. Fans also tend to spend a lot of money inside the ground, buying match programs, eating and drinking, and visiting the club shop where they can buy merchandise. In grounds holding 60,000 spectators or more, it can add up. In the 2006–07 season, Manchester United raised $166.5 million in matchday revenues alone. Sales of hats, books, jerseys, and other merchandise are also very important. Teams bring out three or more complete uniforms every season and can sell tens of thousands of these items. Some manufacturers pay large sums of money to a club for the right to make the uniform.

Money Box

Top five shirt sponsors in Serie A (2006-07)

CLUB	SPONSOR	COST FOR THE SEASON
Juventus	Tamoil	$33 million
AC Milan	Opel	$13.5 million
Internazionale	Pirelli	$10.35 million
Siena	Monte dei Paschi	$9.74 million
Fiorentina	Toyota	$6 million

Source: *SportWeek*

Soccer and the Media

The soccer media includes television, radio, web sites, magazines, and newspapers. They bring news to readers, viewers, and listeners, and put millions of dollars into the sport.

Broadcasting Rights

Television, radio, cell phone, and Internet companies spend fortunes to gain the rights to broadcast soccer matches. At the start of the 2008–09 season, French soccer signed a deal worth $810 million every year with Canal Plus and Orange for the rights to show games. A similar deal for matches in the English Premier League is worth approximately double that. These sums are enormous, and on other continents, the figures are much smaller. The richest club in Morocco, Raja Casablanca, for example, earned a total of just $5.16 million from broadcasting, ticket, and commercial sales in 2007.

Money Box
Juventus is one of the most famous clubs in Italy, yet for some home matches, it gets only a little more than 20,000 fans watching a match live at its ground. Over 60 percent of the club's income each year comes from broadcasting rights.

Broadcasters around the world pay millions of dollars to show the biggest matches, such as the final of the UEFA Champions League, which saw English clubs Manchester United and Chelsea play each other in 2008.

Commentary and Comment

The sports media commentate on live matches and review old games, as well as preview upcoming matches. Soccer is a sport that thrives on opinion. Which player is best? Which team will succeed? Opinions, match reports, and interviews with players and coaches fill many pages of newspapers and occupy hours of radio and television programs. Newspapers, television, and radio all provide work for retired players and some current players. Top soccer players' words and actions are followed in the media and reported across the world. Many players find the attention hard to deal with, but it is part of being a global soccer star.

> ***"Sometimes, I'd like to have a conversation with a friend in a restaurant without feeling I'm being watched. At this rate, I will have to go on holiday [vacation] to Greenland. But maybe the Eskimos would know me."***
>
> Spanish striker, **Fernando Torres**, on the pressures of fame and the media

Sports photographers line the edge of a field and stand behind the goals, hoping to catch an important action shot from a match that they can sell to a photograph agency, sports web site, newspaper, or magazine.

Players and Agents

Today's soccer players can earn millions of dollars every year from salaries, sponsorships, and advertising. Nearly all of the top players have agents who negotiate contracts and deals with clubs and sponsors on the players' behalf.

Rich Rewards

Back in 1909, the English player George Parsonage was banned from playing soccer for life. His crime was to ask for a £50 ($3,890 today) signing fee when he joined a new soccer club. Today, top players are multimillionaires with contracts paying more than $180,000 per week. The best can double their salaries through contracts with sportswear and other companies who pay the players to advertise their products. Although women's soccer falls behind the men's game financially, the best female players can still earn substantial sums from companies sponsoring them. Marta Vieria da Silva from Brazil is one of the highest earners in women's soccer. Including her sponsorship deal with the sports clothing company, Puma, she is believed to earn more than $45,000 per month.

A huge advertising billboard showing the German goalkeeper, Oliver Kahn. Sportswear manufacturer Adidas paid Kahn to use this image in the run-up to the 2006 World Cup in Germany.

> *Alongside my agent, Sir Alex Ferguson has been the most important person I've ever known in my career.*
>
> Manchester United's **Cristiano Ronaldo**

In 2008, Brazilian attacker Robinho signed for the English club, Manchester City. His agent negotiated a weekly salary of $176,400.

Soccer Agents

A player's agent is usually paid a percentage of the player's earnings, so the bigger the deal for the player, the more the agent will earn. As a result, agents are always pushing for better deals for players and have become a powerful force in the modern game. Some people have been critical of the agents' role, believing that agents' demands have helped to drive salaries up and unsettle players into leaving one club for another.

Money Box

Top 10 biggest earners in 2008

1.	**David Beckham** (L.A. Galaxy, United States)	**$44.5 million**
2.	**Ronaldinho** (AC Milan, Italy)	**$34.6 million**
3.	**Lionel Messi** (Barcelona, Spain)	**$32.9 million**
4.	**Cristiano Ronaldo** (Man United, England)	**$27.9 million**
5.	**Thierry Henry** (Barcelona, Spain)	**$24.1 million**
6.	**John Terry** (Chelsea, England)	**$19.9 million**
7.	**Michael Ballack** (Chelsea, England)	**$19.8 million**
8.	**Ronaldo** (Internazionale, Italy)	**$19.1 million**
9.	**Kaka** (AC Milan, Italy)	**$18.4 million**
10.	**Steven Gerrard** (Liverpool, England)	**$18 million**

Source: *France Football Magazine*, 2008

Transfers

Soccer clubs change their squads of players by buying and selling players. These transactions are called transfers.

Reasons for Moving

Soccer players are transferred for many reasons including money, their performances, and their relations with the coach. Clubs may sell a player they would like to keep if a large enough offer is made by another team. A club chairman or board of directors decides whether to sell or keep a player, but when a player wants to leave, this can cause problems. Players may wish to move to another club for a higher salary, to move back to their home country, or to increase their chances of winning major competitions.

ON THE BALL

In 2004, Maribel Dominguez was bought by Mexican club, Celaya. She was the first woman to be transferred to a men's professional team. However, FIFA blocked the move.

Nicolas Anelka of France proved to be a bargain for the English club Arsenal. In 1997, he was bought for $900,000 and then sold three years later to Real Madrid of Spain for $41 million.

Rising Prices

The first recorded transfer was Alf Common's move from Sheffield United to Sunderland for £520 ($75,000 today) in 1902. From the 1950s, prices for the leading players began to rise. The first £1 million ($1.8 million) transfer was Giuseppe Savoldi's 1975 move between Italian clubs Bologna and Napoli, while Jean-Pierre Papin became the first £10 million ($18 million) player when he moved from Marseilles of France to AC Milan of Italy in 1992. Today, the richest clubs worldwide spend $36 million on players, and build teams worth millions.

Zinedine Zidane (left) in action for France. Even though he retired from the game in 2006, Zidane remains the world's most expensive player following his move from Juventus of Italy to Spanish club Real Madrid in 2001.

Money Box

Top five most expensive transfers (to end of 2008)

PLAYER	FROM	TO	FEE
Zinedine Zidane	Juventus (Italy)	Real Madrid (Spain)	$82.1 million
Luis Figo	Barcelona (Spain)	Real Madrid (Spain)	$66.6 million
Hernan Crespo	Parma (Italy)	Lazio (Italy)	$63.9 million
Robinho	Real Madrid (Spain)	Manchester City (England)	$62.1 million
Gianluigi Buffon	Parma (Italy)	Juventus (Italy)	$58.7 million

Source: *World Soccer* and *The Times*

The Demand for Players

The demand for new and better players to boost a soccer club's results is enormous. Some countries allow player transfers to occur only in short periods of the year, known as transfer windows.

Loan Signings

Many clubs cannot afford to buy expensive players. Instead, they rely on borrowing players from other clubs. The club loaning the player hopes that that player will build experience by playing regularly.

Loans can often last for just a few games or weeks, or even for a whole season. Often, a clause is put in the loan contract, stopping the player from playing against their original club should the two teams meet. Some loan players later transfer permanently to their new clubs.

ON THE BALL

In 2007-08, 158 professional players left Brazil and 98 left Argentina to play their soccer abroad, most of them moving to Europe.

The Argentinian player Javier Mascherano joined the English club Liverpool on loan from West Ham in February 2007. Liverpool eventually bought him during the 2008–09 season.

Clubs go to great lengths to sign or develop young talent. Freddy Adu started his career at Major League Soccer team D.C. United in 2004. At the time, he was one of the world's youngest professional players, making his debut at the age of just 14.

> *I don't think that Europe will produce too many [new] players. The big ones will come from Africa and South America, which is why I do so much work in Brazil and Argentina.*
>
> Leading soccer agent,
> **Pini Zahavi**

Player Contracts and Movement

Players will usually sign a contract, binding them to a club for a period of time. At the end of that time, they are free to move to another club. Many clubs choose to sell players who are nearing the end of contracts cheaply rather than let them go for free at the end. On the other hand, many players will wait until the end of their contracts and then move to other clubs for free. Because the new clubs have not had to pay millions of dollars to the old clubs, they can afford to pay the players a much higher salary. European clubs usually pay the highest salaries, attracting players from all over the world. For example, two thirds of the players at the 2004 African Cup of Nations played their club soccer in Europe.

Going Global

Soccer is played in almost every country on the planet. Yet, many people are trying to promote soccer in places where business and soccer have rarely mixed, particularly in Africa, Asia, and Oceania.

ON THE BALL

The A-League in Australia has a salary system where each club has a set amount to spend on 19 of its players' wages. The wages of the club's 20th player can be unlimited.

Expanding Influence

The rise of television has brought the major leagues of Europe into homes all around the planet. As a result, major European clubs, such as Real Madrid and Manchester United, and players such as Cristiano Ronaldo and David Beckham have become famous brands. The clubs have tried to exploit this interest with tours and matches around the world. Organizations such as FIFA have also promoted the sport worldwide with lots of different schemes and by holding competitions in Africa, Asia, and North and South America.

Michael Essien of Chelsea controls the ball during his club's tour of Malaysia in 2008.

David Beckham playing for the MLS club, L.A. Galaxy. Beckham is arguably the world's most famous soccer player and, away from the pitch, is used to advertise a wide range of products in dozens of countries around the globe.

> ***"Asia holds huge potential for clubs hoping to expand their brand and business. There is incredible interest in the sport, the teams, and the players. Our hope is that when someone in places like Korea, Japan, or China thinks about American soccer, they think about the Galaxy."***
>
> Former President and General Manager of L.A. Galaxy, **Alexei Lalas**

New Leagues and Partnerships

In the past 15 years, several countries have tried to improve their elite or top soccer teams and players by starting a professional league. In Japan, the J-League has boomed in popularity since it began in 1993, as has MLS in the United States, whose games began three years later. The world's newest professional men's league, the A-League in Australia, began in 2005. Many major European teams have also formed partnerships with foreign clubs. For example, the Dutch club, Ajax, partly owns the South African club, Ajax Cape Town.

Changing Fortunes

Soccer is hugely competitive and this sees some teams rise and others fall over the seasons. With so much money involved, the pressures are enormous.

Rise and Fall

Some teams have experienced a huge rise in their fortunes. La Paz FC was only formed in 1989, but has become one of the best teams in the Bolivian league. In contrast, some teams can fall even more quickly. In 2001, the English club Leeds United was in the Champions League semifinal. Yet, within a few years, financial problems forced them to sell some of their best players and they were relegated twice.

ON THE BALL

Some leagues deduct points from a club when it goes into administration. The financially troubled English club, Luton Town, started the 2008-09 season on minus 30 points.

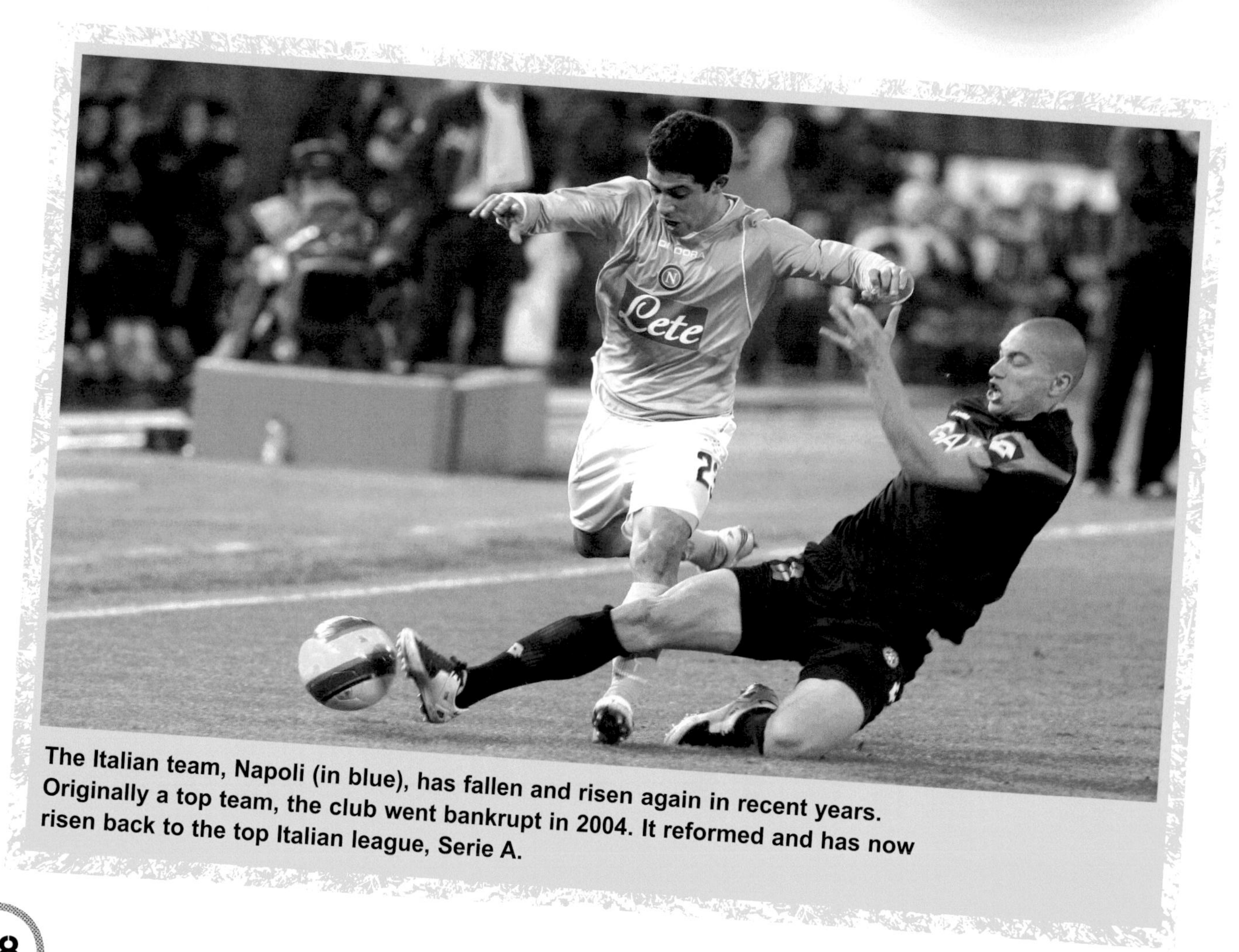

The Italian team, Napoli (in blue), has fallen and risen again in recent years. Originally a top team, the club went bankrupt in 2004. It reformed and has now risen back to the top Italian league, Serie A.

Poor performances bring pressure on players and coaches. The Italian coach Roberto Donadoni (left) was dismissed after Italy's poor showing at Euro 2008, even though the team had won the World Cup two years earlier.

> *"Unfortunately, on our continent we have other priorities like health, education, and development, which are consuming our budget."*
>
> Angola national soccer team coach, **Luis Oliveira Goncalves**

In Trouble

Struggling clubs are under great pressure to succeed. On very rare occasions, this can lead to clubs cheating by trying to fix the results of matches. Bernard Tapie, the former chairman of French club Marseille, was sent to jail in 1997 for bribing referees. In 2006, a major investigation into match-fixing at Italian Serie A clubs saw AC Milan docked points and kicked out of the Champions League, and Italian champions Juventus were docked points, stripped of their league title, and immediately relegated to a lower division.

What It Takes To Be...

A Club Boss

Alexei Lalas

Lalas was a strong central defender who played for the United States team at the 1992 and 1996 Olympics and the 1994 World Cup. During his career, Lalas gained experience of world soccer playing in Ecuador and Italy, before becoming a fans' favorite at a number of MLS clubs. A spell as an analyst on television followed before appointments as general manager of three MLS clubs, where he was responsible for the day-to-day running of the clubs' operations.

Career Path

- 1994: First American player in recent times to play for an Italian Serie A club.
- 2004: Appointed General Manager of the MLS club, San Jose Earthquakes.
- 2005: Became President and General Manager of New Jersey MetroStars.
- 2006: Resigned to become General Manager of the Los Angeles Galaxy.
- 2008: Left Los Angeles Galaxy and returned to work as a soccer analyst.

Alexei Lalas played an important role in David Beckham's move from the Spanish club Real Madrid to the Los Angeles Galaxy in 2007.

Glossary

agent someone who negotiates on a player's behalf, ensuring that they get the best deal from clubs and sponsors.

amateur someone who plays a sport for fun and is not paid for doing so.

coach someone who just works with the players, deciding who should play and what tactics to use, but who does not get involved in any business aspects of the soccer club.

league a group of teams that play each other to decide their standing in a league. The team that wins the most stands at the top and the team that loses the most sits at the bottom, and may be relegated to a lower league.

manager someone who oversees the running of a soccer team, deciding which players play and which tactics to use, and also getting involved in some of the business decisions, such as which players to buy and sell.

merchandise clothing, toys, flags, and anything else that a soccer club can put its name, colors, or logo on and sell to fans to raise money.

professional someone who is paid for playing a sport.

season the continuous run of games over an entire year.

season ticket a ticket that allows a fan to watch all of the games at a team's home stadium throughout an entire season.

sponsorship When a company pays to use a club's logo or a player's name or face to promote its products.

Further Reading

Soccer: The Ultimate Guide to the Beautiful Game
by Clive Gifford (San Val, 2004)

The Everything Kids' Soccer Book
by Deborah W Orisfield
(Adams Media, 2009)

The Kingfisher Soccer Encyclopedia
by Clive Gifford (Kingfisher, 2006)

Web Sites

Due to the changing nature of Internet links, PowerKids Press has developed an online list of Web sites related to the subject of this book. This site is updated regularly. Please use this link to access this list:
http://www.powerkidslinks.com/sos/business

Index